My Writing Journal

By

_____

For my work in progress

_____

Copyright Meredith Bond August, 2019
All rights reserved.
No part of this book may be reproduced in any form or by any electronic or mechanical means including information storage and retrieval systems without permission in writing from the publisher, except by a reviewer who may quote brief passages in a review.

Formatting by Anessa Books

For more information please go to
servesyouwrite.meredithbond.com

Introduction

Dorothy Parker once famously said, "I hate writing. I love having written."

Very few writers actually enjoy writing. It's hard! Some people love the outlining of a book. That initial rush of a new idea, creating the characters, figuring out the complicated plot twists and turns. Others enjoy the editing process, molding their raw words into a story with conflict, crafting sentences into poetry in prose.

This book is here to help you through that, to help you actually write and finish the book in a minimalistic way. It's based on years of my own writing experience, teaching writing for ten years both in person and online, and talking to writers.

A quick word about the layout of each journal page: Obviously the date is the day that you wrote (usually that day that you're filling in the page). Where it says "Written" that can be the number of words you wrote, the number of pages, or the amount of time you spent writing—however you track your writing.

Writing notes about what you did that day will show how productive (or not) you've been. Then noting down what you will write the next time you sit down will help you to get straight to work, the next time you sit down to write.

You'll find help getting started on writing your novel with the "Getting Started" worksheet and on creating your main characters with the Character worksheets. If you need detailed information on the worksheets, you'll find it in my introductory writing

book, **Chapter One**. If you'd like more worksheets, check out my shop on Etsy at
https://www.etsy.com/shop/GetWriting.

If you need further help getting started writing or with accountability—keeping your writing moving forward—don't hesitate to contact me or check out my writing coaching website,
http://servesyouwrite.meredithbond.com.

Introduction: tl;dr

I don't know about you, but I love the concept of tl;dr—too long; didn't read. So here's a super-brief summary of what you need to know to use this book:

- Use the following worksheets to help you get started writing your novel.

- The pages are—mostly—self explanatory: In the "Written" spot, fill in either the number of words you wrote that day, the number of pages or the amount of time you spent writing depending on how you like to keep track of your writing progress.

- Use the stars to track how well you did that day.

Questions? Find me at servesyouwrite.meredithbond.com.

That's it! Enjoy!

When starting a book

Project Title:_____

What's the kernel idea? The spark? _____
_____

Character #1
Internal Goal, Motivation, and Conflict:

They want_____
because _____ but
_____ therefore
_____.

Character #1

Name_____

External Goal, Motivation, and Conflict

They want_____
because _____ but
_____ therefore
_____.

Unique characteristics of this person _____
_____

What is their wound? And how does it shape their life? _____
_____

What's important to them? _____
_____

How do they react to a crisis? (run away, face it down, think it through)_____
_____

What's the worst thing that can happen to this person? _____
_____

Character #2
Name_____
Internal Goal, Motivation, and Conflict:
They want_____
because _____ but
_____ therefore
_____.

Character #2
External Goal, Motivation, and Conflict
They want_____
because _____ but
_____ therefore
_____.

Unique characteristics of this person _____
_____
What is their wound? And how does it shape their life? _____
_____
What's important to them? _____
_____
How do they react to a crisis? (run away, face it down, think it through)_____
_____
What's the worst thing that can happen to this person? _____
_____

Antagonist's
Name_____
Internal Goal, Motivation, and Conflict:
They want_____
because _____ but
_____ therefore
_____.

Antagonist's
External Goal, Motivation, and Conflict
They want_____
because _____ but
_____ therefore
_____.

Unique characteristics of this person _____
_____

What is their wound? And how does it shape their life? _____
_____

What's important to them? _____
_____

How do they react to a crisis? (run away, face it down, think it through)_____
_____

What's the worst thing that can happen to this person? _____
_____

What makes them lovable _____
_____

General Plot Questions

What is the story question? (the overall question that the protagonist(s) must have answered by the end of the book. Ex: Will Dorothy ever get home?)
_____
_____

What's at stake? _____
_____

Where's the sense of urgency? (What will happen if the question isn't answered?) _____
_____

Plot out the Narrative Structure

Inciting incident (what motivates the entire story):
_____
_____
_____

Major Turning Point (moving the protagonist toward their goal): _____
_____
_____

Point of No Return (when the protagonist realizes how difficult it will be to reach their goal):
_____
_____

Crisis (the point when all seems lost): _____
_____
_____

Resolution: _____
_____

Character Examination Worksheet #1

Physical Traits

Name: _____

Age: ____

Hair color, texture, length: _____

Eye color, size, shape: _____

Body type: _____

Distinguishing marks or scars: _____

How to do they speak that is particular to them?
_____

Favorite words, sayings, phrases, exclamations:
_____

Personality Traits

Adjective:	Noun:	Irony:	Verb:

Character Traits

Internal Goal	Internal Motivation	Internal Conflict
External Goal	External Motivation	External Conflict
Strength	Worst Fear	Deep Secret
Identity	Potential	Values (3)
Wound	Belief	Vulnerability

Character Examination Worksheet #2

Physical Traits

Name: _____

Age: _____

Hair color, texture, length: _____

Eye color, size, shape: _____

Body type: _____

Distinguishing marks or scars: _____

How to do they speak that is particular to them?
_____

Favorite words, sayings, phrases, exclamations:
_____

Personality Traits

Adjective:	Noun:	Irony:	Verb:

Character Traits

Internal Goal	Internal Motivation	Internal Conflict
External Goal	External Motivation	External Conflict
Strength	Worst Fear	Deep Secret
Identity	Potential	Values (3)
Wound	Belief	Vulnerability

Character Examination Worksheet #3

Physical Traits

Name: _____

Age: ____

Hair color, texture, length: _____

Eye color, size, shape: _____

Body type: _____

Distinguishing marks or scars: _____

How to do they speak that is particular to them?
_____

Favorite words, sayings, phrases, exclamations:
_____

Personality Traits

Adjective:	Noun:	Irony:	Verb:

Character Traits

Internal Goal	Internal Motivation	Internal Conflict
External Goal	External Motivation	External Conflict
Strength	Worst Fear	Deep Secret
Identity	Potential	Values (3)
Wound	Belief	Vulnerability

Character Examination Worksheet #4

Physical Traits

Name: _____

Age: ____

Hair color, texture, length: _____

Eye color, size, shape: _____

Body type: _____

Distinguishing marks or scars: _____

How to do they speak that is particular to them?
_____

Favorite words, sayings, phrases, exclamations:
_____

Personality Traits

Adjective:	Noun:	Irony:	Verb:

Character Traits

Internal Goal	Internal Motivation	Internal Conflict
External Goal	External Motivation	External Conflict
Strength	Worst Fear	Deep Secret
Identity	Potential	Values (3)
Wound	Belief	Vulnerability

Secondary Characters

Name:_____
Age:____
Physical Description: _____
Relationship to hero/heroine: _____
Goal: _____
****

Name:_____
Age:____
Physical Description: _____
Relationship to hero/heroine: _____
Goal: _____
****

Name:_____
Age:____
Physical Description: _____
Relationship to hero/heroine: _____
Goal: _____
****

Name:_____
Age:____
Physical Description: _____
Relationship to hero/heroine: _____
Goal: _____
****

Character Notes

Start writing no matter what. The water does not flow until the faucet is turned on.

—Louis L'Amour

"Anyone who says writing is easy isn't doing it right."

--Amy Joy

Date: __/__/__
Written: _____
Written Today: _____

Writing Next: _____

☆ ☆ ☆ ☆ ☆

☆ ☆ ☆ ☆ ☆

Date: ___/___/___
Written: _____
Written Today: _____

_____
_____
_____
_____
_____
_____
_____

Writing Next: _____

_____
_____
_____
_____
_____
_____
_____
_____
_____
_____
_____
_____

"You want to be a writer, don't know how or when? Find a quiet place, use a humble pen."

--Paul Simon

"If the book is true, it will find an audience that is meant to read it."

— Wally Lamb

Date: __/__/__
Written: _____
Written Today: _____

Writing Next: _____

☆ ☆ ☆ ☆ ☆

"I think all writing is a disease. You can't stop it."
— William Carlos Williams

Date: __/__/__
Written: _____
Written Today: _____

_____
_____
_____
_____
_____
_____
_____
_____

Writing Next: _____
_____
_____
_____
_____
_____
_____
_____
_____
_____
_____
_____
_____
_____
_____
_____
_____

☆ ☆ ☆ ☆ ☆

"I can shake off everything as I write; my sorrows disappear, my courage is reborn."

— Anne Frank

Date: ___/___/___
Written: _____
Written Today: _____

Writing Next: _____

☆ ☆ ☆ ☆ ☆

An professional writer is an amateur who didn't quit.
—Richard Bach

"Don't try to be different. Just be good. To be good is different enough."

--Arthur Freed

Date: ___/___/___
Written: _____
Written Today: _____

_____

Writing Next: _____

☆ ☆ ☆ ☆ ☆

☆ ☆ ☆ ☆ ☆

Date: __/__/__
Written: _____
Written Today: _____

Writing Next: _____

"People say, 'What advice do you have for people who want to be writers?' I say, they don't really need advice, they know they want to be writers, and they're gonna do it."
— R.L. Stine

"I believe myself that a good writer doesn't really need to be told anything except to keep at it."

— Chinua Achebe

Date: __/__/__
Written: _____
Written Today: _____

Writing Next: _____

☆ ☆ ☆ ☆ ☆

"Don't bend; don't water it down; don't try to make it logical; don't edit your own soul according to the fashion. Rather, follow your most intense obsessions mercilessly."
- Franz Kafka

"The road to hell is paved with works-in-progress."

– Philip Roth

Date: ___/___/___
Written: _____
Written Today: _____

Writing Next: _____

☆ ☆ ☆ ☆ ☆

"An artists' job is to surprise himself. Use all means possible."
— Robert Henri

Date: __/__/__
Written: _____
Written Today:_____

_____
_____
_____
_____
_____
_____
_____
_____

Writing Next: _____

_____
_____
_____
_____
_____
_____
_____
_____
_____
_____
_____
_____
_____
_____
_____

☆ ☆ ☆ ☆ ☆

☆ ☆ ☆ ☆ ☆

Date: / /
Written: _____
Written Today: _____

Writing Next: _____

"The road to hell is paved with adverbs."

— Stephen King

"I don't care if a reader hates one of my stories, just so long as he finishes the book."

— Roald Dahl

Date: __/__/__
Written: _____
Written Today: _____

_____
_____
_____
_____
_____
_____
_____
_____

Writing Next: _____

_____
_____
_____
_____
_____
_____
_____
_____
_____
_____
_____
_____
_____
_____

☆ ☆ ☆ ☆ ☆

"We are all apprentices in a craft where no one ever becomes a master."

—Ernest Hemingway

Date: ___/___/___
Written: _____
Written Today: _____

_____
_____
_____
_____
_____
_____
_____

Writing Next: _____

_____
_____
_____
_____
_____
_____
_____
_____
_____
_____
_____
_____
_____
_____
_____

☆ ☆ ☆ ☆ ☆

"The greatest part of a writer's time is spent in reading, in order to write; a man will turn over half a library to make one book."
—Samuel Johnson

Date: __/__/__
Written: _____
Written Today: _____

_____
_____
_____
_____
_____
_____
_____
_____

Writing Next: _____

_____
_____
_____
_____
_____
_____
_____
_____
_____
_____
_____
_____

☆ ☆ ☆ ☆ ☆

> "Half my life is an act of revision."
>
> -- John Irving

"All you have to do is put one word after another, and remember how great it feels to be a writer."

--Stephanie Lennox

Date: __/__/__
Written: _____
Written Today: _____

Writing Next: _____

☆ ☆ ☆ ☆ ☆

☆ ☆ ☆ ☆ ☆

Date: / /
Written: _____
Written Today: _____

_____
_____
_____
_____
_____
_____
_____

Writing Next: _____

"There are no laws for the novel. There never have been, nor can there ever be."

— Doris Lessing

"I do not over-intellectualize the production process. I try to keep it simple: Tell the damned story."

—Tom Clancy, WD

Date: ___/___/___
Written: _____
Written Today: _____

Writing Next: _____

☆ ☆ ☆ ☆ ☆

"I would advise anyone who aspires to a writing career that before developing his talent he would be wise to develop a thick hide."
—Harper Lee, WD

Date: ___/___/___
Written: _____
Written Today: _____

Writing Next: _____

☆ ☆ ☆ ☆ ☆

☆ ☆ ☆ ☆ ☆

Date: ___/___/___
Written: _____
Written Today: _____

_____
_____
_____
_____
_____
_____
_____
_____

Writing Next: _____

_____
_____
_____
_____
_____
_____
_____
_____
_____
_____
_____
_____
_____
_____
_____

"Let the world burn through you. Throw the prism light, white hot, on paper."

—Ray Bradbury, WD

"Remember: Plot is no more than footprints left in the snow after your characters have run by on their way to incredible destinations."

— Ray Bradbury, WD

Date: __/__/__
Written: _____
Written Today: _____

Writing Next: _____

☆ ☆ ☆ ☆ ☆

"It's none of their business that you have to learn how to write. Make them think you were born that way."
--Ernest Hemingway

Date: __/__/__
Written: _____
Written Today: _____

_____
_____
_____
_____
_____
_____
_____

Writing Next: _____
_____
_____
_____
_____
_____
_____
_____
_____
_____
_____
_____
_____
_____
_____
_____
_____
_____

☆ ☆ ☆ ☆ ☆

"Writing is not necessarily something to be ashamed of, but do it in private and wash your hands afterwards."
— Robert A. Heinlein

Date: ___/___/___
Written: _____
Written Today: _____

Writing Next: _____

☆ ☆ ☆ ☆ ☆

☆ ☆ ☆ ☆ ☆

Date: ___/___/___
Written: _____
Written Today: _____

_____
_____
_____
_____
_____
_____
_____

Writing Next: _____

_____
_____
_____
_____
_____
_____
_____
_____
_____
_____
_____
_____
_____
_____

"There is only one plot—things are not what they seem."
—Jim Thompson

"I think all writing is a disease. You can't stop it."
—William Carlos Williams

Date: __/__/__
Written: _____
Written Today: _____

_____
_____
_____
_____
_____
_____
_____

Writing Next: _____

_____
_____
_____
_____
_____
_____
_____
_____
_____
_____
_____
_____
_____

☆ ☆ ☆ ☆ ☆

"The most beautiful things are those that madness prompts and reason writes."

—Andre Gide

Date: ___/___/___
Written: _____
Written Today: _____

Writing Next: _____

☆ ☆ ☆ ☆ ☆

When I say work I only mean writing. Everything else is just odd jobs."

—Margaret Laurence

Date: __/__/__
Written: _____
Written Today: _____

Writing Next: _____

☆ ☆ ☆ ☆ ☆

"The difference between almost the right word and the right word... is the difference between the lightning bug and the lightning. --Mark Twain

Date: ___/___/___
Written: _____
Written Today: _____
_____
_____
_____
_____
_____
_____
_____

Writing Next: _____
_____
_____
_____
_____
_____
_____
_____
_____
_____
_____
_____
_____
_____
_____
_____
_____
_____

☆ ☆ ☆ ☆ ☆

"I always start writing with a clean piece of paper and a dirty mind."

— Patrick Dennis

Date: __/__/__
Written: _____
Written Today: _____

Writing Next: _____

☆ ☆ ☆ ☆ ☆

☆ ☆ ☆ ☆ ☆

Date: ___/___/___
Written: _____
Written Today: _____

Writing Next: _____

"When writing a novel a writer should create living people; people, not characters. A character is a caricature."
—Ernest Hemingway

"Keep a small can of WD-40 on your desk—away from any open flames—to remind yourself that if you don't write daily, you will get rusty."

—George Singleton

Date: __/__/__
Written: _____
Written Today: _____

Writing Next: _____

☆ ☆ ☆ ☆ ☆

"You don't actually have to write anything until you've thought it out. This is an enormous relief, and you can sit there searching for the point at which the story becomes a toboggan and starts to slide."

—Marie de Nervaud

Date: __/__/__
Written: _____
Written Today: _____

Writing Next: _____

☆ ☆ ☆ ☆ ☆

"You have to write the book that wants to be written. And if the book will be too difficult for grown-ups, then you write it for children."

—Madeleine L'Engle

Date: ___/___/___
Written: _____
Written Today: _____

Writing Next: _____

☆ ☆ ☆ ☆ ☆

☆ ☆ ☆ ☆ ☆

Date: __/__/__
Written: _____
Written Today: _____

Writing Next: _____

"Substitute 'damn' every time you're inclined to write 'very;' your editor will delete it and the writing will be just as it should be.
— Mark Twain

"If there's a book that you want to read, but it hasn't been written, then you must write it."

--Toni Morrison

"If there's a book that you want to read, but it hasn't been written yet, then you must write it."

— Toni Morrison

Date: __/__/__
Written: _____
Written Today: _____

Writing Next: _____

☆ ☆ ☆ ☆ ☆

"Either write something worth reading or do something worth writing."

— Benjamin Franklin

Date: __/__/__
Written: _____
Written Today:_____
_____
_____
_____
_____
_____
_____

Writing Next: _____
_____
_____
_____
_____
_____
_____
_____
_____
_____
_____
_____
_____

☆ ☆ ☆ ☆ ☆

"No tears in the writer, no tears in the reader. No surprise in the writer, no surprise in the reader."

– Robert Frost

Date: __ / __ / __
Written: _____
Written Today: _____

Writing Next: _____

☆ ☆ ☆ ☆ ☆

"Read, read, read. Read everything -- trash, classics, good and bad, and see how they do it. Just like a carpenter who works as an apprentice and studies the master. Read! You'll absorb it. Then write. If it's good, you'll find out. If it's not, throw it out of the window."

— William Faulkner

Date: __/__/__
Written: _____
Written Today: _____

Writing Next: _____

☆ ☆ ☆ ☆ ☆

☆ ☆ ☆ ☆ ☆

Date: __/__/__
Written: _____
Written Today: _____

Writing Next: _____

"You must stay drunk on writing so reality cannot destroy you."
— Ray Bradbury

"A writer is someone for whom writing is more difficult than it is for other people."

— Thomas Mann

Date: __ / __ / __
Written: _____
Written Today: _____

Writing Next: _____

☆ ☆ ☆ ☆ ☆

"Here is a lesson in creative writing. First rule: Do not use semicolons. They are transvestite hermaphrodites representing absolutely nothing. All they do is show you've been to college."
— Kurt Vonnegut Jr

Date: __/__/__
Written: _____
Written Today: _____

Writing Next: _____

☆ ☆ ☆ ☆ ☆

"Any reviewer who expresses rage and loathing for a novel is preposterous. He or she is like a person who has put on full armor to attack an ice-cream sundae."

--Kurt Vonnegut

"You can make anything by writing." — C.S. Lewis

Date: __/__/__
Written: _____
Written Today: _____

Writing Next: _____

☆ ☆ ☆ ☆ ☆

"Tears are words that need to be written."

— Paulo Coelho

Date: __/__/__
Written: _____
Written Today: _____

_____
_____
_____
_____
_____
_____
_____

Writing Next: _____

_____
_____
_____
_____
_____
_____
_____
_____
_____
_____
_____
_____
_____

☆ ☆ ☆ ☆ ☆

☆ ☆ ☆ ☆ ☆

Date: __/__/__
Written: _____
Written Today: _____

Writing Next: _____

"Writing is like sex. First you do it for love, then you do it for your friends, and then you do it for money."
— Virginia Woolf

"Always be a poet, even in prose."

— Charles Baudelaire

Date: __/__/__
Written: _____
Written Today: _____

_____
_____
_____
_____
_____
_____
_____

Writing Next: _____

_____
_____
_____
_____
_____
_____
_____
_____
_____
_____
_____
_____
_____
_____
_____

☆ ☆ ☆ ☆ ☆

"If my doctor told me I had only six minutes to live, I wouldn't brood. I'd type a little faster."

— Isaac Asimov

Date: __/__/__
Written: _____
Written Today: _____

Writing Next: _____

☆ ☆ ☆ ☆ ☆

"The purpose of a writer is to keep civilization from destroying itself."

— Albert Camus

Date: __/__/__
Written: _____
Written Today: _____

_____
_____
_____
_____
_____
_____
_____

Writing Next: _____

_____
_____
_____
_____
_____
_____
_____
_____
_____
_____
_____

☆ ☆ ☆ ☆ ☆

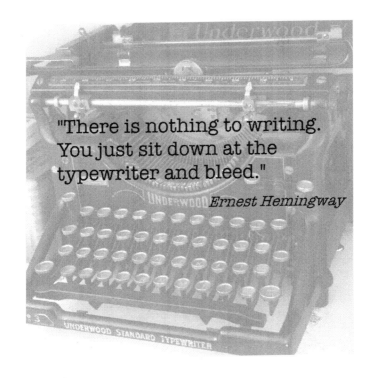

"I write to discover what I know."

— Flannery O'Connor

Date: ___/___/___
Written: _____
Written Today: _____

Writing Next: _____

☆ ☆ ☆ ☆ ☆

"Ideas are like rabbits. You get a couple and learn how to handle them, and pretty soon you have a dozen."

— John Steinbeck

Date: ___/___/___
Written: _____
Written Today: _____

_____
_____
_____
_____
_____
_____
_____

Writing Next: _____

_____
_____
_____
_____
_____
_____
_____
_____
_____
_____
_____

☆ ☆ ☆ ☆ ☆

☆ ☆ ☆ ☆ ☆

Date: __/__/__
Written: _____
Written Today: _____

Writing Next: _____

"Words do not express thoughts very well. They always become a little different immediately after they are expressed, a little distorted, a little foolish."

– Hermann Hesse

"The most valuable of all talents is that of never using two words when one will do."
— Thomas Jefferson

Date: __/__/__
Written: _____
Written Today: _____

Writing Next: _____

☆ ☆ ☆ ☆ ☆

"A blank piece of paper is God's way of telling us how hard it is to be God."

— Sidney Sheldon

Date: __/__/__
Written: _____
Written Today: _____

_____
_____
_____
_____
_____
_____
_____

Writing Next: _____
_____
_____
_____
_____
_____
_____
_____
_____
_____
_____
_____
_____
_____

☆ ☆ ☆ ☆ ☆

"I went for years not finishing anything. Because, of course, when you finish something you can be judged."

— Erica Jong

Date: __/__/__
Written: _____
Written Today: _____

Writing Next: _____

☆ ☆ ☆ ☆ ☆

☆ ☆ ☆ ☆ ☆

Date: ___/___/___
Written: _____
Written Today: _____

_____
_____
_____
_____
_____
_____
_____

Writing Next: _____

_____
_____
_____
_____
_____
_____
_____
_____
_____
_____
_____
_____
_____
_____

"I love deadlines. I like the whooshing sound they make as they fly by."

— Douglas Adams

"You only fail if you stop writing."
                    Ray Bradbury

"Half my life is an act of revision."

— John Irving

Date: __ / __ / __
Written: _____
Written Today: _____

Writing Next: _____

☆ ☆ ☆ ☆ ☆

"Get it down. Take chances. It may be bad, but it's the only way you can do anything really good."

— William Faulkner

Date: _/_/_

Written: _____

Written Today: _____

Writing Next: _____

☆ ☆ ☆ ☆ ☆

"Almost anyone can be an author; the business is to collect money and fame from this state of being."

— A. A. Milne

Date: __/__/__
Written: _____
Written Today: _____

Writing Next: _____

☆ ☆ ☆ ☆ ☆

☆ ☆ ☆ ☆ ☆

Date: __/__/__
Written: _____
Written Today: _____

Writing Next: _____

"When you make music or write or create, it's really your job to have mind-blowing, irresponsible, condomless sex with whatever idea it is you're writing about at the time."

— Lady Gaga

"We are not our writing. Our writing is a moment moving through us."

— Natalie Goldberg

Date: ___/___/___
Written: _____
Written Today: _____

_____
_____
_____
_____
_____
_____
_____

Writing Next: _____

_____
_____
_____
_____
_____
_____
_____
_____
_____
_____
_____
_____
_____
_____

☆ ☆ ☆ ☆ ☆

"If we knew each other's secrets, what comfort we should find." John Churchton Collins

Date: ___/___/___
Written: _____
Written Today: _____

Writing Next: _____

☆ ☆ ☆ ☆ ☆

☆ ☆ ☆ ☆ ☆

Date: __/__/__
Written: _____
Written Today: _____

Writing Next: _____

"I don't care if a reader hates one of my stories, just so long as he finishes the book."

Roald Dahl

"The universe buries strange jewels deep within us all and then stands back to see if we can find them."
—Elizabeth Gilbert

Date: ___/___/___
Written: _____
Written Today: _____

Writing Next: _____

☆ ☆ ☆ ☆ ☆

"...if you don't feel any kind of doubt, there's probably something wrong!"

—Joanna Penn

Date: __/__/__
Written: _____
Written Today: _____

Writing Next: _____

☆ ☆ ☆ ☆ ☆

☆ ☆ ☆ ☆ ☆

Date: __/__/__
Written: _____
Written Today: _____

_____
_____
_____
_____
_____
_____
_____

Writing Next: _____

_____
_____
_____
_____
_____
_____
_____
_____
_____
_____
_____
_____
_____
_____

"Do you need someone to make you a paper badge with the word 'WRITER' on it before you can believe you are one?"

--Stephen King

"Those who do not want to imitate anything, produce nothing."
 -- Salvador Dali

Date: ___/___/___
Written: _____
Written Today: _____
_____
_____
_____
_____
_____
_____
_____

Writing Next: _____
_____
_____
_____
_____
_____
_____
_____
_____
_____
_____
_____
_____
_____
_____

☆ ☆ ☆ ☆ ☆

"Why write? Why breathe?"

--Katherine Mansfield

Date: __/__/__
Written: _____
Written Today: _____

Writing Next: _____

☆ ☆ ☆ ☆ ☆

> "Hear criticism and weight it against your inner truth."
> — Julia Cameron

"Writing a book is a horrible, exhausting struggle, like a long bout of some painful illness. One would never undertake such a thing if one were not driven on by some demon whom one can neither resist nor understand."

--George Orwell

Date: __/__/__
Written: _____
Written Today: _____

Writing Next: _____

☆ ☆ ☆ ☆ ☆

"There is no greater agony than bearing an untold story inside you."
--Maya Angelou,

Date: __/__/__
Written: _____
Written Today: _____

Writing Next: _____

☆ ☆ ☆ ☆ ☆

☆ ☆ ☆ ☆ ☆

Date: __/__/__
Written: _____
Written Today: _____

Writing Next: _____

"Lock up your libraries if you like; but there is no gate, no lock, no bolt that you can set upon the freedom of my mind."

-- Virginia Woolf

"We write to taste life twice, in the moment and in retrospect."
-- Anais Nin

Date: __/__/__
Written: _____
Written Today: _____

Writing Next: _____

☆ ☆ ☆ ☆ ☆

"One day I will find the right words, and they will be simple."
--Jack Kerouac

Date: ___/___/___
Written: _____
Written Today: _____

_____
_____
_____
_____
_____
_____
_____

Writing Next: _____
_____
_____
_____
_____
_____
_____
_____
_____
_____
_____
_____
_____
_____
_____
_____
_____
_____
_____

☆ ☆ ☆ ☆ ☆

"Fantasy is hardly an escape from reality. It's a way of understanding it."

--Lloyd Alexander

Date: __/__/__
Written: _____
Written Today: _____

Writing Next: _____

☆ ☆ ☆ ☆ ☆

"Fiction is the truth inside the lie."
— Stephen King

☆ ☆ ☆ ☆ ☆

Date: __/__/__
Written: _____
Written Today: _____

Writing Next: _____

"Writing is a socially acceptable form of schizophrenia."
--E.L. Doctorow

"After nourishment, shelter and companionship, stories are the thing we need most in the world."

-- Philip Pullman

Date: ___/___/___
Written: _____
Written Today: _____

_____
_____
_____
_____
_____
_____
_____

Writing Next: _____
_____
_____
_____
_____
_____
_____
_____
_____
_____
_____
_____
_____
_____
_____

☆ ☆ ☆ ☆ ☆

"History will be kind to me for I intend to write it."
--Winston S. Churchill

Date: __/__/__
Written: _____
Written Today: _____

_____
_____
_____
_____
_____
_____
_____

Writing Next: _____

_____
_____
_____
_____
_____
_____
_____
_____
_____
_____
_____
_____
_____
_____
_____
_____

☆ ☆ ☆ ☆ ☆

> "Stories may well be lies, but they are good lies that say true things, and which can sometimes pay the rent."
>
> --Neil Gaiman

Date: ___/___/___
Written: _____
Written Today: _____

_____

Writing Next: _____

☆ ☆ ☆ ☆ ☆

"The first draft of anything is shit." --Ernest Hemingway

Date: __/__/__
Written: _____
Written Today: _____

Writing Next: _____

☆ ☆ ☆ ☆ ☆

"A writer is someone for whom writing is more difficult than it is for other people."

--Thomas Mann

Date: __/__/__
Written: _____
Written Today: _____

_____
_____
_____
_____
_____
_____
_____

Writing Next: _____

_____
_____
_____
_____
_____
_____
_____
_____
_____
_____
_____
_____
_____
_____

☆ ☆ ☆ ☆ ☆

"let me live, love, and say it well in good sentences" --Sylvia Plath

Date: __/__/__
Written: _____
Written Today: _____

Writing Next: _____

☆ ☆ ☆ ☆ ☆

"There are three rules for writing a novel. Unfortunately, no one knows what they are."

W. Somerset Maugham

"There is something delicious about writing the first words of a story. You never quite know where they'll take you."
 --Beatrix Potter

Date: __/__/__
Written: _____
Written Today: _____

Writing Next: _____

☆ ☆ ☆ ☆ ☆

☆ ☆ ☆ ☆ ☆

Date: __/__/__
Written: _____
Written Today: _____

Writing Next: _____

"Tomorrow may be hell, but today was a good writing day, and on the good writing days nothing else matters."
—Neil Gaiman

"I write to give myself strength. I write to be the characters that I am not. I write to explore all the things I'm afraid of."
-- Joss Whedon

Date: ___/___/___
Written: _____
Written Today: _____

Writing Next: _____

☆ ☆ ☆ ☆ ☆

"You can't wait for inspiration. You have to go after it with a club."
—Jack London

Date: __/__/__
Written: _____
Written Today: _____

Writing Next: _____

☆ ☆ ☆ ☆ ☆

"Write what you know. That should leave you with a lot of free time."
 --Howard Nemerov

Date: __/__/__
Written: _____
Written Today: _____

_____
_____
_____
_____
_____
_____
_____
_____

Writing Next: _____

_____
_____
_____
_____
_____
_____
_____
_____
_____
_____
_____
_____
_____
_____
_____

☆ ☆ ☆ ☆ ☆

"The purpose of a writer is to keep civilization from destroying itself."

Albert Camus

"So what? All writers are lunatics!"

--Cornelia Funk

Date: __/__/__
Written: _____
Written Today: _____

Writing Next: _____

☆ ☆ ☆ ☆ ☆

"Description begins in the writer's imagination, but should finish in the reader's."

-- Stephen King

Date: ___/___/___
Written: _____
Written Today: _____

_____
_____
_____
_____
_____
_____
_____

Writing Next: _____

_____
_____
_____
_____
_____
_____
_____
_____
_____
_____
_____
_____
_____
_____

☆ ☆ ☆ ☆ ☆

☆ ☆ ☆ ☆ ☆

Date: ___/___/___
Written: _____
Written Today: _____

_____
_____
_____
_____
_____
_____
_____

Writing Next: _____
_____
_____
_____
_____
_____
_____
_____
_____
_____
_____
_____
_____

"Learn the rules like a pro, so you can break them like an artist."
-- Pablo Picasso

"If you can't annoy somebody, there is little point in writing."
--Kingsley Amis

Date: __/__/__
Written: _____
Written Today: _____

Writing Next: _____

☆ ☆ ☆ ☆ ☆

"Great writers are indecent people they live unfairly saving the best part for paper."
-- Charles Bukowski

Date: __/__/__
Written: _____
Written Today: _____

_____
_____
_____
_____
_____
_____
_____

Writing Next: _____

_____
_____
_____
_____
_____
_____
_____
_____
_____
_____
_____
_____
_____

☆ ☆ ☆ ☆ ☆

"One always has a better book in one's mind than one can manage to get on to paper."
--Michael Cunningham

Date: ___/___/___
Written: _____
Written Today: _____

_____
_____
_____
_____
_____
_____
_____
_____

Writing Next: _____
_____
_____
_____
_____
_____
_____
_____
_____
_____
_____
_____
_____
_____
_____

☆ ☆ ☆ ☆ ☆

"When you are in the middle of a story it isn't a story at all, but only a confusion; a dark roaring, a blindness, a wreckage of shattered glass and splintered wood."

-- Margaret Atwood.

Date: __/__/__
Written: _____
Written Today: _____

Writing Next: _____

☆ ☆ ☆ ☆ ☆

"All I need is a sheet of paper and something to write with and I can turn the world upside down."

      Freidrich Nietzche